So Far, So Good

Wit and Wisdom from Our Elders in Times of Adversity

David Lemon, M.D.

Writers Club Press
San Jose New York Lincoln Shanghai

So Far, So Good
Wit and Wisdom from Our Elders in Times of Adversity

Published by Writers Club Press
an imprint of iUniverse.com, Inc.

For information address:
iUniverse.com, Inc.
620 North 48th Street
Suite 201
Lincoln, NE 68504-3467
www.iuniverse.com

ISBN: 0-595-00018-5

Printed in the United States of America

To my parents, Ken and Marge Lemon who died tragically before I really knew them.

Table of Contents

Introduction

I remember the incident only too well. It seems now like it occurred only yesterday, but, in fact, it was 16 years ago. I am a heart doctor, better known as a cardiologist. I'm supposed to know everything there is to know about your heart. Sixteen years ago I thought I did know almost everything. I was in my mid-thirties and had settled into a rigorous and eventful practice. I thought I knew what was "best" for my patients. It was my job to know.

On this particular day I had the unwelcome task of talking seriously with one of my patients, Carl Guenther. Carl was in trouble. He was 70 years old and had suffered a serious heart attack. This had left him short of breath, tired and discouraged. Time seemed to be running out. He had developed a hole in the wall of his heart that separated two of its chambers.

Carl knew he was dying and so did I. I told him that things didn't look so good and tried to console him. It didn't work. His concerned wife was at his side. I outlined the situation and remarked that because of his age, our options were limited.

That's when he let me have it! "Dr.," he screamed, "Don't you ever tell me I'm too old. Do what needs to be done and get on with it."

We did. Carl survived a major life saving operation and lived for sixteen more productive and joyful years. Over that time he reminded me often of our conversation that day. He also changed forever, my thoughts about what it means to be old. As Carl grew older and I grew older, at least one of us became a lot wiser as we aged. I came to appreciate older people and the lessons they taught me about life and just staying alive. I marveled at my 85 year old farmers, housewives, attorneys, and business people and wanted to explore more thoroughly their secrets for long life and happiness. I needed to know as much for myself as for anyone.

After considerable thought and with some trepidation, I decided to develop a questionnaire to explore their secrets. My wife was quite helpful. Together we developed a set of questions that required written responses, not just a yes or no or an "x". My subject population consisted of stable outpatients known to me for at least one year and preferably 80 years or older. I wanted a cohort who trusted me, had been through sickness and had survived. Their perspectives on life, I felt, would be genuine and instructional.

It turned out to be quite a project and took over a year of data collection. In the end, the response to my efforts was heart warming. Over 70% of all patients asked to participate did so willingly. They opened their lives, their beliefs and doubts as well as their hopes and dreams. They sent me photos, clippings, anniversary announcements, graduation pictures, and poems, but mostly they sent me a part of themselves. When I would see them for follow up in the office, most asked how the book was coming and wanted to share a new story or insight. My project became their project.

This book is about them. I enjoyed writing it. I hope you enjoy it also. I think you might just agree with me, "So Far, So Good."

Chapter 1

Growing Old in America

The definition of "being old" has always been relative to who is making the observation. To a four year old, someone eighteen years old is ancient. To someone eighty years old, someone 100 years old is ancient. As we physicians know well, not all eighty year old patients are physiologically the same. Persons who have remained physically and mentally active and have a reason to get up each morning, can go on almost indefinitely. They are resilient and wonderful patients.

The Baltimore Longitudinal Study of Aging has gone a long way in helping us understand the aging process. We are now more readily able to distinguish what happens when we age versus what happens when we are inactive. The two processes are not synonymous. Active elderly persons show very little decline in physical and mental capacity well into the eighth decade. Physically fit octogenarians regularly compete in long distance running events, and get college degrees. Their response to endurance training closely matches their younger neighbors. Resting heart rate decreases, body fat decreases, flexibility improves, and bone density is maintained. It appears that there is no upper limit where these benefits are curtailed.

Elderly persons learn to adapt. Although the capacity for memory decreases, there is no decline in the ability to process data and do sophisticated problem solving. Personality remains stable as we age; we do not become "another person" as we age. If we are rabble rousers as youngsters, we probably will shake a few trees even when we grow old.

As a society we have also changed our definition of being old as our life expectancy has increased. In 1900, the average American could expect to live roughly forty-seven years. In 1999, the life expectancy for Americans is now seventy-two years for males and seventy-nine years for females. In Japan, most citizens will live beyond the age of eighty. Medical science has yet to define how high these averages can potentially reach. Interestingly, there has been no change in the percentage of us living to one hundred years, even though the average life expectancy has continued to increase. Experts tell us that there are a few fortunate individuals who have "selective survival" and evidently are not as susceptible to the usual illnesses to which you and I succumb as we age. It is undeniable that some families have a genetic propensity for long life, not related to the presence or absence of conventional cardiovascular risk factors. It is my opinion that we can expect to see the average life expectancy to continue to increase to at least the mid-eighties in the not too distant future.

Every day we are subjected to conflicting advertising snippets as to the desirability of aging. One moment we glorify youth and vigor, the next moment we see the "Ensure Generation" and the "Centrum Silver" crowd rafting down the Colorado River. No wonder we as a society don't know how to deal with getting old. Age brings with it wisdom, but also the baggage of opportunities lost and dreams never fulfilled.

This much is clear, we as a nation are aging and we have to come to grips with that reality. Individually, I have observed that my patients greatly appreciate the gift of age and value the mere fact they have made it this far. Most accept their lot in life and have few regrets. Simple events take on new meaning. Details become more important. Time slows down. The sun looks a little brighter and the sky never looked so blue. Every conversation with a neighbor can be repeated verbatim to anyone who wants to listen. Cooking dinner isn't just nuisance, but an event. Cutting the potatoes just a certain way and perfectly arranging the salad are paramount. If the meat is overcooked, a hundred explanations are offered as to how that could have happen. It doesn't matter how the election turned out, but it matters a lot more that cousin George found a nice girl and they might just get married.

A good example of the general optimism of older folks is seen in how they respond to the simple question, "How old are you?" Almost always the response goes like this. "Next year I'll be 83." Not, "I'm 82." What better demonstration of optimism in their future could there be?

Don't we revel in the fact that George Burns really did make it to age 100? Could Bob Hope really be almost ninety-five? I could swear I just saw him play golf on TV last week. The passing of "the Chairman of the Board", old Blue Eyes himself, Frank Sinatra elicited a national day of mourning. I'll bet most every American felt pride and wonder when John Glenn recently blasted into space at age seventy-seven.

On the more sinister side, however, lurking just below the surface, is the constant fear of the elderly of being abandoned, discarded, or thought of as no longer relevant. It is most notable in men who have lost their wives, moved into town, or retired from a vigorous, all consuming job. Women who have lost dear friends or children also are susceptible. I see it expressed in my patients' protestations to me as we outline treatment plans for their heart problems. We euphemistically refer to this in the profession as "age-based" decision making. To me it is very much more. I hear it every day. Listen to what these people say. "Doctor, I don't want to be a burden." "I don't want to be hooked up to a machine." " I don't like to take medicine, it takes away my independence." "I don't want to go to a nursing home." " Who will take care of my spouse?" "Why live? All my friends are dead." Each of these statements echoes their feelings of being left alone or of not fulfilling their responsibilities. Each of these statements reflects an elderly person's value system and what determines quality of life for them. Each of these statements also reflects major societal questions concerning how we treat our elders.

Complicating this further is the attempt to politicize age and put a dollar value on life. We are not so subtly told that resources are wasted on the elderly. In fact, carefully done studies have shown this is not the case. Costs of acute care for hospitalization after age seventy-five actually go down on a case by case comparison versus younger patients. In fact, the case mix, that is, why elderly persons are admitted to the hospital, seems to reflect a less costly basis once patients achieve a ripe old age. Care is usually given in the community hospital, not in the Ivory Tower. End of life decisions are being made appropriately and inappropriately aggressive therapy has thankfully become less commonplace. Clinical pathways of care, case managers, and long term home based follow-up is now the norm rather than the exception.

We as a society must be careful to evaluate each problem associated with aging realistically. Promises that cannot be kept, should not be made. Social Security will continue to be a hot button issue—who pays? how much? who gets it? Medicare versus Medicaid—are they equivalent? Are they welfare? Is one group more worthy? Have old people paid their dues? Schools versus nursing homes, Pre-World War II versus Post-World War II, depression mentality versus the "me" generation, this is the challenge we face.

We all have a bit of gerontophobia (fear of aging). The popular press will only continue to increase our anxieties as we age. The options will increase, the number of people affected will continue to swell and intelligent and compassionate answers must be found. We must remember, as we look into the eyes of our elders, we see our own reflections because tomorrow "they will be us".

It is time to take a glimpse into the lives of John and Martha Van Holden (fictional) and see what it means to be old and to have a heart problem. John will represent the composite of a typical elderly male patient as he makes his way through the health care system.

Chapter 2

John Goes to the Doctor

It's Monday morning and as usual I'm running late. I'm supposed to see patients in the office starting at 9:00 a.m., as I do every Monday. To get finished on time, I've started making hospital rounds one half hour earlier than usual. So far, no serious problems have upset my plan. I know the first office patient will be waiting when I get there. My "caffeine fix" from five cups of coffee is wearing off and I'm already sleepy. I hope that the patients I see today will be stimulating. I hate to make patients wait for me. I feel I owe them my time. Many of them travel seventy miles to see me. The least I can do is listen to them and try to help make their lives a bit more comfortable.

Sure enough, the chart for the first patient is sitting in the office, ready for me to study before I visit with my patient.

Blaine, my nurse, walks in and cheerfully announces, "You're gonna like this guy." This sounds encouraging and I review the information he has obtained from the patient.

My patient's name is John Van Holden. He lives on a hog farm southeast of Des Moines. He is eighty-two years old and still farms. In Iowa, if your last name starts with "Van", that pretty well tells me where you live now or at least where you started out eighty-two years ago. It also tells me you have probably worked hard all your life, paid your bills and taxes, and believe in God. This might sound like a stereotype, but it is true.

Things haven't gone well for John the last few years. In 1995, hog prices were great. He got $0.40 out of every dollar for which pork sold at the supermarket. Like many other Iowa farmers, he expanded his operation, bought a new Chevy truck and even took a five day vacation. Then the Asian Crisis hit the world economy, demand for pork dried up, prices hit rock bottom, and John was not sure how he could make ends meet. I knew this was a factor in John's reason for coming to see me.

The chart says John has "a touch of diabetes" and is semi-retired. A semi-retired farmer means that instead of owning all the farm, he has sold or rented some of it to a corporation or handed it over to his kids. Instead of just worrying about hogs and corn, he now has also to worry about his son making it as a farmer. Now he works twelve hours a day instead of sixteen hours a day and he drives the tractor instead of the combine. I know something must really be bothering John, since farmers don't worry about little things like their own health. In fact, during planting season or during the two week harvest marathon, not even a heart attack will make them come in to the hospital. That stuff can wait. One last thing I notice before I go in to talk with John is that he is 5'8" tall and weighs 210 pounds. By some life tables, that makes him obese. In Iowa it does not. He has earned every pound of that over the last fifty years.

I open the door to the examining room and there sits John and his wife, Martha. Before I can even say a word or extend my hand, John pipes up, "How you doing, Doc? I hope I'm not wasting your time. The wife made me come in here. There's nothing wrong with me." Right away I know he is my kind of guy.

I am continually amazed how patients show concern for "the doctor". Here is this hard working man, away from his work, who has traveled forty miles, and has gotten up a 4:00 a.m. to feed the hogs and he is worried about wasting my time.

I've learned that when John says, "THE WIFE", not "my wife", it is not a put-down, but, just the opposite. He has placed her above all others and she is "the one". Even though John would hate to admit it, in his weakest moments, he might just agree that "THE WIFE" is his best friend and soul mate.

John is a generous sized man. He is still wearing his yellow cap that says, "Born Country" on the front. His face is wind burned and looks like a plaster mold. His grin is infectious. His hands are large and callused, but the skin is soft; his handshake is solid and genuine. He is wearing clean, but well worn coveralls. Part of him bulges over the sides. On his feet are "Air Nikes", strangely out of place and probably purchased on sale by Martha just for this occasion. I hope he did not buy them just to see me. I hope that I can help him feel better.

Martha sits at John's side. Her skin is worn, but she is attractive and I wonder what she looked like fifty years ago. She does not seem to want to make eye contact with me, but sneaks a worried glance toward John. She is wearing a blue scarf, a plaid dress, and what look like new walking shoes. Clutched in her hand is a small note pad with a pencil, both look well used. I know that these are to take notes, to remind John that the doctor said this and the doctor said that. She will also use her notes to report back to the rest of the family. As time goes on, she will use my spoken words to coerce John into walking the straight and narrow. She will cross things out and add little bits on the margins, all in an effort to remain in control of what is to come.

In Iowa, family is everything. Going to the store is a family decision. Children are always children regardless of their ages, marital status, or social standing. The "boy" may be sixty years old, but try telling that to John or Martha. I know that the only reason that John is here to see me is that Martha has laid down the law.

John begins to tell me his story, but not without prompting. "Doc, it's no big deal. I have just been getting a little indigestion. Seems to come on at the darndest times. The Maalox just doesn't seem to work. Maybe I need a stronger antacid. Funniest thing, I get it when I'm just doing my chores. If I stop, it goes away. Last couple of nights it just wakes me up. If I belch, it goes away. It doesn't seem like the heartburn I used to get. Maybe I'm just a wimp. I get so tired I feel like all I want to do is take a nap."

Martha pipes up, "John, tell the doctor about yesterday. I saw you leaning against the barn! You couldn't even make it back to the house. I had a good mind to haul you in to the hospital yesterday. Lord knows! You'll be a dead man before you'll admit you're not indestructible."

This exchange goes on for two minutes, back and forth; they forget I'm even in the room. Finally, John gives up. "Okay, woman, you win, let him cut me up and throw me to the hogs. I'm not worth much anymore anyway."

I've heard enough. I know that John is in trouble. I know it is not his stomach, but his heart that holds his fate. What I am going to recommend will change his life forever.

There is no way to sugar coat the news. John needs an angiogram. This is a heart test to look at the arteries that feed the heart muscle. We call these arteries the coronary arteries. They can become plugged up with cholesterol causing loss of blood flow to parts of the heart and resulting in a heart attack with death of heart muscle and often death of the patient. John's symptoms suggest that this is a rapidly progressing process and that the situation is unstable. The angiogram should be scheduled soon.

As expected, John spends the next five minutes telling me why he cannot find time for the test. Who will feed the hogs, milk the cows, drive the tractor? Couldn't this wait until all the crops are in? The negotiations continue without much progress. Once again Martha comes to my rescue and ends the dialogue with a fiat. "John, you will do what the doctor says, when he says to do it and that's that." Decision made.

John sheepishly relents to her verbal onslaught and negotiates two more days of freedom before the test. I outline what is in store for him, start him on a medication called a beta-blocker, and usher him slowly toward the door. He assures me that nothing is really wrong and that this is a waste of time. Martha tells him to hush up.

I hope John will return. People usually do return for their tests. What they fear is losing control of their lives. A spouse like Martha helps a guy like John look death in the eye and laugh. The verbal exchange allows them to avoid the reality of having to deal with the fear of death and their vulnerability.

We will pick up the story of John and Martha again a bit later.

Chapter 3
Why Do We Live So Long?

Why do some people live so long? The answer to this question so far has eluded medical science. Many theories have been hypothesized and tested, but so far they are just that, theories. Each theory has its vocal proponents and data to back it up. I think my patients have become experts on the issue, since they are living proof. Each of the more than eighty patients I studied had very strong feelings about what contributed to their longevity.

First, though, let us look at the science of aging. Everyone agrees that as we age the metabolism of the body slows down and that wear and tear eventually take their toll. Our caloric needs are reduced, our bones become less dense, our muscle mass decreases and our reflexes slow. It is also clear, however, that the rate of deterioration is in part under our control and in part genetically determined. In fact, habitually active individuals age more slowly. Aerobic capacity, or the ability to perform work shows little deterioration over a twenty to thirty year span of time from age forty to sixty-five in those who remain physically active. It is inactivity, not age that has to be sorted out. Less than twenty percent of American adults exercise regularly. Those who exercise regularly, maintain a stable body weight, retain flexibility, and have fewer co-morbid or health related conditions that shorten lifespan. Men and women over age eighty routinely compete in long distance running events, climb high mountains, and do white water rafting down the Colorado River. Some senior citizens like John Glenn even get to re-explore the wonders of space with ho apparent adverse effects.

Studies in mammals show that calorically restricted but nutritionally sound diets allow animals to live fifty percent longer than matched animals allowed to eat freely. I have a feeling this will prove to be true for humans as well, but I'm not sure I want to volunteer for that study.

Social scientists have suggested that continued learning, forced social interaction, scheduled activities, and a "reason for getting up" all contribute to long life. I see this phenomenon everyday. Healthy older people don't want to retire. They don't want to slow down. They want to contribute. Their wisdom and experience replace a mind that was like a sponge. Complex activities become habit, as veteran Minnesota Vikings quarterback, Randall Cunningham says, "the game slows down," and the correct choices become more evident. Humor takes on a gentler tone and perspective smoothes out the day to day fluctuations of life.

Medical science deserves some credit for slowing down the aging engine. It is not all the heroic things, but the public and environmental health interventions that over time have been most beneficial. Clean water, vaccinations against disease, adequate housing, adequate disposal of sewage, public education—all these have separated the more fortunate parts of the world from the not so fortunate.

This is all very interesting, but let us see what the real experts, my patients, have to say on these matters. First, let us examine what a good spouse does for an individual. In my survey, one hundred percent of my patients were married or had been married at one time or another during their lives. Over sixty percent still had their spouses alive and living with them, even though they, themselves were over eighty years old. A living and loving spouse was especially important to men. This is best illustrated by one simple question I asked them. "Who is your best friend?" Eighty percent of the male respondents said it was their wives. Only twenty percent of the women listed their husbands as their best friends. Women tended to mention their adult children or female friends more often. Elderly men and men in general have less well developed socialization skills and seem to be more dependent upon their wives for emotional support and friendship. It is not infrequent for men to die within one year following the death of their wives. I believe their hearts are truly broken and their will for living is gone. They can only drink so many cups of coffee, read the paper so many times, or check on the crops so many times. Without their lifetime "buddy" the men just fade away. Women, on the other hand, tended to have multiple prearranged social groups, ongoing relationships with adult children, and well established "busy work" to keep their minds and hands busy. I believe this to be a marked difference in the aging of men and women in America.

Clark Shaw expresses this sentiment well when he talks about his wife, telling me, "I attribute my long life to the love and loyalty of a truly good person, my wife." Ruby Peterson says, "I have lived a long life because I have a loving husband and a caring family." Florence Baily, age 91, said she attributed her long life to "having a husband I liked and loved and raising a family who loved and respected me." Barney Stangl meant it when he told me, "I love my wife as much today as I did when I married her fifty years ago."

Sentiment aside, something genuine is going on here. It is the sense of belonging and being needed and needing the support of someone else. Older Iowans may not show much emotion to the casual observer, but it is the shared work and struggles as well as the calmness of a long life together that keeps them going. It is the stability and predictability that foster a sense of peace. This seems to be in direct contrast to the values and lifestyle being thrust upon us everyday.

What better tribute can a man give to his wife than the following quote in response to a question about taking congregate meals. "They want me to take congregate meals. I told them she's (his wife) been cooking for me for sixty years and that will always be good enough for me." Dwight Gates told me, "I would like to live long enough to take care of my wife as long as she lives."

I found that no particular occupation conferred the gift of longevity. My male patients were fairly equally distributed between farmers, blue collar workers, service related, and professionals. I found no significant trend in my female patients, either. What seemed consistent was the theme that hard work, keeping busy and having a positive attitude were important. In fact only four patients failed to mention hard work as important. The word "retirement" was never mentioned. Kicking back and taking it easy was never mentioned. Professionals mentioned mentoring their younger colleagues, farmers helped their sons with crops and women were all involved in their local charities, churches, or with grandchildren.

Bernadine Keller is representative of the idea of work and keeping busy. She says, "I have to still tell them I'm all booked up." She worked at the College of Nursing at the University of Iowa until age seventy-four. She currently volunteers for six different organizations.

Marion Crossly told me, "Hard work has helped; I always had a job to report to." Margaret Osborn said, "I am never bored and there never seems to be enough time to do the things I want and need to do." I think Ed Olney hands out some pretty good advice. "If you plan ahead, stay busy and work hard, you will stay out of trouble and live longer." Pretty hard to argue with that.

Maynard Reese, a renowned wild life artist and recent recipient of an unexpected heart bypass operation said, "I work almost as hard as I ever did. I keep working because the only time I am completely relaxed and completely happy is when I'm painting. I don't want to give that up and I won't as long as I can move a brush." Personally, I hope he never stops painting.

I almost never tell my patients to retire or slow down. I tell them it is my goal, God willing, to keep them going, pedal to the metal, as long as possible. This builds their confidence and reinforces the idea that living, not illness, is what I want them to emphasize. Most elderly patients are relieved to hear his. A tense frown is replaced by a smile and an "I told you so" nudge to the worried spouse. Grandpa really can still drive the tractor; it's okay to have coffee every morning with the guys and it's even okay to throw down a couple of beers on the weekend.

Contrary to previous studies I have read, owning a pet was not important. Only twenty percent of my patients owned pets. I imagine this is because in Iowa, with close and extended families, real people, rather than animals, are companions as we grow older. My patients seemed to be too busy to feed Fido, anyway.

Some of my patients used the phrase, "clean living" or "not smoking" as a factor contributing to long life, but I was struck how infrequently this came up. Only one male patient listed modern medical advances as a major factor in his longevity. As a physician, perhaps I should be humbled by their assessment, but I think what I'm hearing is that they, the patients are trying to control their own destinies. The ever increasing reliance on alternative medicine, self help programs on television or the Internet, and the backlash against HMO's is part of the same message. More money is currently spent on alternative medical care than on medical care using traditional primary care physicians. It is therefore not surprising to see this "self help" philosophy extended to our elders.

How do older people come to grips with their own heart disease? How do they deal with the real prospect of death? The predominant response to these questions was an intense sense of being grateful just to be alive and to have been given more time with family and friends. Almost half of my patients say they just don't worry about it. Almost twenty percent said their heart problems had no effect on their lifestyle. Only two patients admitted openly that fear or worry was a daily driving thought that dominated their lives.

I find this denial of fear or worry totally different from what I hear from the forty to sixty-five year old crowd that stream through my office. They haven't "made it" yet. There are too many bills to pay, kids to send to college, and the fear of down-sizing and job loss. Will these people survive the next twenty-five years to make it to the "promised land?" Or were the now eighty year olds somehow able to deal with things differently when they were fifty-five?

Maxine Seaton displays uncanny wisdom as she tells me, "I don't talk or complain to my friends about it (her heart). I live each day calmly. I deal with it by not even thinking about it." Ruby Chongo told me, "Doc, you gotta laugh." Alma Kutchin quipped, "I have a pink sweatshirt and in teal colors it says, 'YES I CAN'. I wear it often." Maxine Roberts' advice to us rings true, "Be optimistic and always look at the good things instead of the bad." Carl Brommer meant it when he related to me, "my heart problem, it made me appreciate everyday and everything." My world traveler patient, John Peterson, who is never at a loss for words quipped, "Live each day as if it's your last because it may be."

Accepting life's vagaries seems to be a consistent theme. It is almost like a gentle breeze whispering to be quiet and steady. Mabel Waller said it best, I think. "There are a few things I'd like to do but if I don't get them done it will be okay. I think we should all live each day as it comes and not worry too much about tomorrow." At age ninety-two, Ione Hoyt almost makes one want to cry when she tells me she doesn't want to go to a nursing home. "I can take care of myself," she says. She is blind, but "I can still dance around my walker as well as I ever could." Hortense Harman, age ninety, who recently died in her sleep, told me, "I learned young that you have to take care of yourself." Well she did take care of herself and everyone around her also. Up until the time she died she read daily to friends and acquaintances and I'm sure was miffed at dying at such an inopportune time!

Belief in God was universal among my patients. Only one professed no belief in a Higher Being. Ruth Patterson summed up the sentiment nicely to me in an eloquent, yet simple phrase. "I worry about nothing and pray about everything." Pretty good advice I think. Spirituality is a topic in itself and we will study this more closely later, but let's check back on John and Martha and see if John has returned for his heart test.

Chapter 4

John Needs a Heart Test

It is 7:30 a.m. and the cardiac catheterization lab is already paging me. Ardie, our head nurse and traffic cop for the lab is quickly getting the show on the road. She tells me that my first patient to be catheterized for the day is John Van Holden. I remember John. At least he has survived the last three days. Ardie sounds a bit apprehensive on the phone and tells me that John had to use a nitroglycerin pill for chest pain this morning after he got up at 4:40 a.m. to feed the hogs. I remark that I am not surprised and that I am glad his family has persuaded him to come in for his angiogram. In fact, I would learn later that John had been awakened each of the last three nights with chest pain. He only came in when his son assured John that all chores would be handled and that he would inform John daily of any changes on the farm.

The angiogram is the diagnostic test we use to look at the anatomy of the coronary arteries that supply blood to the heart. A small catheter is inserted in the femoral artery in the groin area. The catheter is threaded up the large artery called the aorta under x-ray guidance and into each of the coronary arteries. We humans have a left coronary with two main branches and a right coronary artery. An iodine based material is injected through the catheter and into the arteries and motion pictures are taken as the "dye" flows through the arteries. Any narrowing in the arteries from atherosclerosis can be localized and measured for severity of narrowing. On the basis of the degree of narrowing, the number of narrowings, and location of the narrowings, a treatment plan can be developed. This is the test John is about to experience.

As John is wheeled into the cath lab, I briefly chat with him. His wife, son, and daughter shadow his every move. Martha, his wife, has a tight grip on his hand and the ever present handkerchief clutched in her other hand. She is trying to be brave, but the love of her life is in trouble and she knows it. John, on the other hand, is trying to be the tough guy and pretends this will all be a big picnic. He bellows out to me, "Hope you got a good night's sleep, Doc. Does your work come with a ten year warranty? By the way, how many of these angiograms have you done?" I jokingly assure John that I have been up all night and that this is the first angiogram I have ever done. This pre-battle banter is standard fare for all of us.

We all want our doctors to be smart and get sleep and be at the top of their game. We want to confer on them some magic so they will take care of us. I do the same thing whenever I see my orthopedic surgeon about my bum knee. The consequences of failure are too much for us to handle. I sometimes wonder if I would have the courage to let someone perform an angiogram on me knowing all about it the way I do.

John is placed on the cath lab table—a narrow, uncomfortable, hard, cold moveable device. He is strapped to the table so he can't move and ECG monitoring electrodes are placed on his chest so we can watch his heart rhythm. An IV is already infusing sugar water into his arm. Oxygen is applied to his nose via small plastic prongs. Next the groin area is shaved and cleansed with a pink sterile solution and the whole area covered with a disposable sterile drape. The area over the femoral artery is then deadened with Lidocaine, a local anesthetic. By this time, John has become very quiet; the Valium we have given him has mellowed him out and the gravity of the situation has begun to sink in. I am dressed in a scrub suit, lead apron, blue sterile gown, gloves and a mask. The room is filled with all kinds of high tech equipment. People scurry about preparing for the case to begin. I often wonder what that all looks like for patients who are frightened and have had Valium. Do they hallucinate? What do they hear? Are they praying? Would I be so brave?

The lights go down and the show begins. I insert the catheter in the leg artery and advance it into the coronary arteries with no difficulty. By this time, John is snoring peacefully.

Martha and the family are in the waiting room, huddled in a corner. About now, both of John's adult children are feeling guilty that they haven't spent more time with their dad. Each family member seems to recall a favorite story about dad and they remark to each other how much more important these memories are right now.

Meanwhile, in the cath lab, things are going smoothly. The pictures we are getting seem clear and no complications occur. As predicted, we find that John has severe narrowings in all of his coronary arteries. We also find evidence of prior heart damage. I know right then that John will probably need a bypass operation.

A few minutes later, I nudge John and ask him if he is all right. He wonders if we have started the study yet. I tell him that he was a "party pooper" and slept through the whole thing. I also tell him he really snores loudly. He promptly falls back to sleep. I know he will be in "La-La-Land" for at least the next two hours. He is moved from the cath table, wheeled into the recovery area and reattached to a heart monitor.

John's family is ushered into the lab so that I might show them the actual pictures I have just taken of John's heart. I have learned over the years that it is more effective to show people what I see rather than tell them what I see. I also try not to get too technical. "Just the facts," as Joe Friday used to say. No one cracks a smile. Martha has tears in her eyes. She doesn't hear a word I am saying. "Is he okay, Doc? Do you have to cut him open? Don't let him go home; he will never come back." I assure her that he is resting comfortably and try to put a positive spin on his upcoming surgery. This takes some convincing, but after ten minutes, the family begins to loosen up a bit and John's son tries to reassure his mother. Martha finally dries her eyes, lets out a big sigh and tells me if it is the Lord's will, then John indeed will be okay. She tells the kids to call all the relatives and pass the word. Each family member now takes his turn being assertive and optimistic, but I've seen it too many times; they are scared to death.

I tell Martha to get a snack, take a walk and in an hour or two, we'll both sit down with John and go over the details. If he is receptive to the idea of a bypass operation, I can have one of the surgeons talk to him about the operation.

Meanwhile, in the recovery room, John is blissfully snoring away, oblivious to what is in store for him. Two hours later, he slowly wakes up, complains that his groin aches and asks for some lunch. He brags that the angiogram was no big deal. The clamp on his groin is removed and he can sit up about twenty degrees. I show John a computerized version of his arteries and point out the areas of blockage and what it all means. He tries to keep things light and asks if he can still feed the hogs this afternoon. Martha just stares at the ceiling in disbelief. Eventually, though, he starts asking questions and it is obvious that reality has set in. He asks Martha what she thinks and Martha wisely tells him it's his heart, but she will support any decision he makes.

I am glad Martha has responded to John this way. It is very important for patients to make this decision on their own. They must decide, not the spouse. If things go bad and John dies, who is left to take all the guilt if he has been coerced into having the surgery? You guessed it—Martha. I firmly believe that a positive attitude going into surgery is THE most important factor in a patient's recovery. If it's got to be done—do it. Don't look back. Don't second guess yourself. You will survive! A relaxed and resigned attitude to upcoming surgery is essential.

Martha assures John that she has seen the pictures. He looks at her and says, "Maybe they ought to just shoot me—after all, what good is an 80 year old washed up hog farmer." Martha ignores his comment and tells him he won't get away from her that easy. His eyes gloss over, then he seems to refocus, makes a fist and says, "Doc, lets go for it! I trust you. Get those chest crackers in here and tell me what's going to happen. But promise me, if things go wrong, you won't leave me hooked up to one of those machines." I assure him I won't.

One of our heart surgeons comes in to speak with John. He is thorough, not rushed and very down to earth. The family is impressed. John gains confidence. It is suggested that surgery should not be delayed. John tries for one last shot at control and insists he needs two days to get his affairs in order. The surgeon understands this emotion and relents. I intensify John's medical regime before he leaves and ask him to have someone else feed the hogs for now. As he walks out the door, he reminds me that he still has two days to change his mind, but I know he won't. Martha scolds him and reassures us he will be back at the arranged time, even if she has to bind and gag him to get the job done.

As doctors, we sometimes don't realize the implications of what we say and the endless number of statistics we quote to support our arguments. For instance, a five per cent chance of dying during surgery sounds like a reasonable risk, doesn't it? That's one chance in twenty. Well, if you are the patient, "your" statistic is either I live or I die. Maybe you are that "one in twenty". We pride ourselves on informing patients of their options and risks, but sometimes we need to think like a patient. Eventually, all of us come to this point in our lives. Many of my patients have never been seriously ill; not once in their eighty plus years. Yet, I stand there and calmly tell them they may die as a consequence of what I recommend. If I dwell on this thought too long, I often become very troubled. Am I saying the right thing? Is my judgment sound? Some days you are right. Some days you are wrong.

When we meet John again later, we will see how he does during his heart bypass operation.

Chapter 5
We Are What We Believe

We are most human not when we cling to life, but when we let it flow through us. This is a paraphrase of a passage our minister, Reverend David Ruhe often uses. I am beginning to understand better what he means. My patients have been my teachers. Life for them flows; it has continuity and rhythm, with interesting detours along the way. Above all, they profess a profound gratitude for just being alive with an appreciation directed to our Maker. God is very much alive in Iowa. God is not an abstract principle to my patients, but an ever present friend and THE most important factor in their long and eventful lives. Only one patient interviewed said he did not believe in God. How refreshing! Time and again, God defined their existence and reason for living. Quotes from the

Bible were frequently used to answer my questions. All patients seemed to make a clear distinction between religion and being religious and believing in God. Being religious was viewed as a social, not spiritual concept. Being religious was what your neighbors did, believing in God was for your soul. Two patients went so far as to specifically state they had a profound belief in God, but did not attend church nor view themselves as religious. This is quite interesting to me because using church attendance as a measure of spirituality may vastly underestimate the real importance of God in the lives of our countrymen.

When I asked Maxine Roberts who her best friend was, she told me it was Jesus Christ. She told me her faith had seen her through five serious operations without fear, the death of a one year old son in an automobile accident, and the death of her daughter at age forty-four from breast cancer. I think this indeed is a true test of one's faith.

Hazel Courtney said, "I think my long life is by the grace of God." Notice, she did not say because of a low fat diet or because of her doctor or because of luck. No, it was the grace of God, that unearned blessing bestowed upon us and manifest in my patients as a calm demeanor and a relaxed smile. Notice the grace and dignity of Hazel Anzel, age 101, who told me, "I would appreciate living a little longer so I can see my great granddaughter become a little older."

Again and again, the same words were used—appreciation, thankfulness, gratitude, faith, and belief. Only three patients expressed any anger or resentment about their illness or being victimized by bad luck. This is quite remarkable since most of them will indeed die as a consequence of their heart disease. Does this represent simple resignation to their fate, which is a passive or defeatist approach, or does it represent a proactive, optimistic attitude toward a manageable problem? My guess is that it is the latter.

Listen to the joy that Alice Couch, age 83 expresses when she says, "I always say music makes my heart sing. I pray that if I have hurt someone, they will forgive me and I also will forgive them." Is this the voice of an 83 year old? It sounds to me like someone who is young at heart, very much alive and in touch with her feelings.

I observed that positive attitude and expressions of thankfulness were not confined to either gender, nor related to former occupation, social status, or wealth. Louie Krick, a retired dentist, was almost too good to be true when he told me, "It is a wonderful world out there, make the most of it." That phrase would make even the beloved Jimmy Stewart proud. Clark Shaw recounted, "Every day of my life I begin with a prayer of gratitude and thanksgiving." Lawrence McMullen, in his closing remarks to me epitomizes a humble, nonpretentious attitude; "I would like at this time to thank all who have helped me through life. I just feel that if I treat people right, trust in God, and leave liquor alone, I'll make it."

As I probed further, I became intrigued by my patients' views on death, afterlife and leaving a loved one behind. When you're eighty years old, this is not just interesting speculation, but an ever present consideration with all its attendant consequences.

Most patients seemed reluctant to face the issue of death or to talk about it early in the course of their illness, but once a diagnosis had been established, and a plan of care outlined, they generally accepted the idea of dying quite calmly. Don Schissel, a physician friend of mine, recently died after a protracted course with heart disease and prostate cancer. I had occasion to visit with him at length one week before he died. He was obviously in pain and very weak, but kept his smile and seemed so calm and at peace. He had told me earlier in the year, "I am uncertain as to life after death, although I accept whatever comes on faith." Even in his dying days, he stayed interested in life and displayed not a trace of bitterness or regret.

Maxine Seaton is another long term patient of mine who I respect and admire. She is always calm, accepting, and upbeat. Her response to the question about death is representative; "I don't know if I'm afraid of dying. I know I don't want to (die). I still have a zest for life." Remember, these are the words of an eighty-two year old lady with severe disability, not a starry eyed teenager. It further reinforces my belief about how we view life as we age. Life is precious, regardless of what the calendar says.

There was a small contingent of patients who just could not stomach the thought of death and used humor to keep the thought manageable. Dorothy Primm said, "Never gave it a thought." Mary Robinson, age 84, remarked, "I'm not interested in trying it right now, but it could prove interesting. Maybe there are a lot of spirits around." John Muir said, "I'm not ready to die because I enjoy life too much." I wonder if they are practicing a bit of sophisticated denial in these statements. By making light of death, they are in a sense, not acknowledging it and therefore don't have to worry about it.

One theme that cropped up again and again was the concept of continuity between life and death. Death was viewed by most as just another stop along the way so, "What's the big deal?" I think Frances Baarda was trying to tell me this when she said, "God has taken care of me so far; when my time comes, I'll just go. I just take it as it comes."

Florence Bailey, age 90, is one of my favorite patients. When she visits me in the office, I come away from our visits knowing that she has given me more than I can ever give her. Life for her is pretty straight forward. Things are pretty cut and dried. She says, "Death is really a fact of life and I accept that fact." So far, she has dealt with everything just fine, thank you!

Julia Ellis, age 83, has an attitude toward death that mirrors her attitude toward life and is inspiring. She told me, "I am not really afraid of death. I know one day when it's my time to go, I'll be ready. I've lived a good life and still will until it's time to go with God. I'm sure glad things happened the way they did."

Another recurrent theme was the fear of leaving loved ones alone and vulnerable. Several regretted that things would be left "undone" or just a "little incomplete". "How will my death affect my wife? Who will take care of the farm? Have I done everything I can to see that my affairs are in order? I just wish I had more time."

Harold Depenning, age 85, is not above a little bargaining when he says, "I'm not quite ready to die. I would like to see the 21st century. I want to give my family the things I have worked for."

Don Peterson says he may be a bit afraid of dying "because of what I will leave undone, worry about leaving my wife alone if she survives me and religiously because I have not done enough good in the world." I guess I'm privileged to know Don, wouldn't you agree?

I think a consistent picture emerges. I see a group of "elderly" individuals, profoundly grateful for life, strong in their beliefs, and very articulate in their ability to express their value systems. Death is ever present for these individuals and not to be feared, but to be faced the same way that they have faced life. Above all, the picture is one of a group of persons who seem relaxed and at peace with themselves and their surroundings. They seem to have accepted whatever comes with an optimistic attitude. Whether this attitude has made it possible for them to live so long or has evolved because they have lived so long, we will probably never know for sure. This is an important issue for us as a society to further explore. As we run faster and faster and work harder and harder to stay afloat, our mainstream culture seems at odds with this mindset. It seems unlikely to me that the next "over 80 years" generation will have such a serene attitude toward life.

It's time to check back on John and see if his operation will be a go.

Chapter 6

John Needs Surgery

The day of surgery has arrived, John's day of continued life or death. Either this will be his last day here on his beloved farm or the beginning of a new life with all of its possibilities. The last two days have been hard for him. Since I told John he needed to have a bypass operation, each moment has become more precious to him. Even the act of shaving, which he always thought was such a bother, has become special. Every daily chore has now become a treasured ritual. Yesterday he noticed how pretty his wife looked, how she smiled when she nagged him and how good that second cup of coffee tasted. He couldn't bear the thought of never seeing her again. Would she be okay? Maybe she would be "too okay". Maybe nobody would even miss him. In short, John realized, probably for the very first time, how valuable life really was and how much he wanted more of it. He said a quiet prayer and noticed how much better he felt.

On the morning of surgery, John and Martha checked into the hospital's outpatient registration area promptly at 6 a.m. He had insisted on driving and almost intentionally missed the interstate turn off toward the hospital. He took a nitroglycerin tablet and put it under his tongue as the registration nurse checked his vital signs. By the time he had finished filling out all the papers he was feeling better.

John and Martha were ushered into a small cubicle and he was ordered to give up his clothes, even his underwear. He felt cold and vulnerable. A pretty, young nurse came in and introduced herself, but he didn't catch her name and couldn't even crack a smile or think of a clever line. All of this time, he and Martha couldn't even look at each other; both knew what was at stake. All of the statistics didn't matter now. John would live or John would die; he would have a chance for that second cup of coffee each morning or Martha would have only memories. John felt very small. He wished that he were more religious. He wished he had told Martha how much she meant to him.

This awkward interlude was broken when the anesthesiologist strode in and introduced himself. He was reassuring. He exuded confidence and told John he had the best heart surgeons in town. He reviewed for Martha what would happen and what to expect. He told her where the waiting room was and that she would be updated as the surgery progressed. He inserted an IV line into John's wrist and checked his arm band identification a second time. He joked that John's veins were as big as garden hoses. He guessed that John's coronary arteries would also be big and easy to operate. Martha smiled for the first time.

Soon an orderly from the operating room appeared. He checked John's ID band and helped him onto the cart. As is usual, the gown John was wearing was too small and missing a draw string, leaving his rear end flapping in the breeze. John was sweating and nauseated. His chest felt tight. He was scared. Martha's handkerchief was now just a wadded up ball in her clenched fist. John reminded Martha to have the kids feed the cattle and remembered that the electric bill needed paying. Still, their eyes didn't meet. The cart pulled away and Martha touched his shoulder. He gave her the thumbs up sign and finally looked her in the eye and smiled.

John was wheeled directly into the operating room and placed on a table. Like the cath lab, this table was also cold, hard and narrow. The overhead lights seemed very bright to John and lots of people were scurrying about. He felt more calm and confident now. His body was painted from stem to stern with an orange disinfectant. He vaguely remembered hearing the anesthesiologist say something and felt a small sting as another IV was placed in his neck vein. Ever so gradually, he slipped into a dreamless sleep.

By this time, the surgeon had arrived and John's wind pipe had been intubated with a tube to help him breathe. This was attached to a mechanical ventilator. The large, complicated looking artificial bypass machine was wheeled in and the show began.

An assistant surgeon worked quickly on John's left leg, exposing a two foot area along the inside of his left calf. After about fifteen minutes, a long piece of vein was retrieved and placed into a preservative solution. This would serve as the bypass graft material around John's own clogged arteries. Four separate pieces of vein would be used as well as one of John's own chest arteries, called the internal mammary artery.

Meanwhile, John's chest was opened with an electric saw, splitting the breast bone down the center to give good exposure. He was hooked up to the bypass machine so that his body would be supplied with oxygen while the heart was stopped.

The surgery itself was routine. John's coronary arteries were indeed quite large and made the sewing a surgeon's dream. The whole surgery, start to finish, took only two hours. Martha was kept informed by hospital volunteers every half hour. At the end of the operation, Dr. Soltanzadeh met with Martha in the waiting area and updated her. He was upbeat. He told her that John would look horrible for a while, but not to be alarmed. She breathed a sigh of relief and thanked him. The children now had all arrived to join Martha and they all filed down to the cafeteria. Each member had their favorite story to tell about Dad. Martha was only quiet.

Two hours after the surgery was complete, John was beginning to breathe on his own in the Coronary Care Unit. The nurse assessed his condition and checked his vital signs closely. Yes, he could move all his extremities. His grips were equal on both sides. The pupils of his eyes reacted normally to light. He even tried to smile, which is some trick with a breathing tube down your wind pipe.

Martha was allowed to sit at his bedside for a few moments. To her, he looked dreadful. He was ashen and cold to the touch. Tubes stuck out of every orifice, making him look a little like a porcupine or a vodoo doll. He smelled like astringent soap. His eyes were closed. A large monitor above his head displayed all his vital signs and a repetitive beeping sound tracked his heart beat.

She grabbed his hand and squeezed. To her surprise he squeezed back. His eyes opened and he looked at her. John was beginning to wake up. He was disoriented and felt heavy and groggy. He realized he could not talk. Everything was a blur. He saw a person, but couldn't tell who it might be.

Martha was ushered back to the waiting room to update the rest of the family. They had a hundred questions and she tried to remain calm and in control. She felt very tired and as if all of this were a dream or some surreal play and she was just one of the players. She laid down on a cot and quickly drifted into a well earned nap.

Early in the afternoon I stopped by the coronary care unit to check on John's progress. I reviewed his flow sheet; everything seemed in order. His post operative electrocardiogram showed no changes. The nurses assured me that neurologically he was fine.

A cardiologist's worst nightmare sending his or her patient to the OR is a post-operative stroke. We all breathe easier when the patient awakens. I guess it all relates back to something I learned in medical school about "doing no harm". If we can't make you better, at the least, we don't want to make you worse. I really believe that. At least this time, we were lucky.

I peered through the door and saw Martha sitting there, holding John's hand with her right hand. In her left hand was a Bible and she was reading a passage. I then remembered, as I need to be reminded, what all of this means. For some reason, I was overwhelmed with the sense that this is why I became a doctor. This was real. These were not cases or clients or marketing objects, but real people. If John got better, then I would feel better. We all would win.

A brief digression is in order here. Families see in their loved ones more than we as doctors see. We as doctors often only see problems, cases, solutions and outcomes. Families see memories, promises kept, and a future to share. We see wrinkles, fat and old age. They see endurance, "huskiness", and a good appetite.

At age eighty, my patients can still help "the old folks" at church. In their own minds, they are not eighty, really, it's the other guy over there who is eighty. "I" am forever young. Mom and Dad are still Mom and Dad whether they are age thirty or age eighty. The kids are still kids even though they may be sixty. The grandkids still need to be cared for and taught and spoiled. Age doesn't change the basic relationships or values, only the facade may whither a bit. Success and failure are not age discriminate. Meaning to life is not age dependent. Love can only grow stronger over time and with age. All of this is seen in Martha's simple holding of John's hand.

Day two post-op dawned brightly, at least weather wise. John had indeed survived his ordeal and he was indeed neu-rologically intact. The tube was removed from his throat, the drainage tubes removed from his chest and the Foley catheter removed from his bladder. The breathing machine was wheeled from the room. He still had two IV lines in place. He was bruised from head to toe and felt awful. Going ten rounds with Mike Tyson would be easier than this, he observed. He felt drugged, nauseated, and weak. Each breath seemed like someone was stabbing him in the chest. All of his visitors smiled and said how great he looked. He just wanted to puke.

During the day, his heart rhythm becomes unstable. He has developed atrial fibrillation, a common problem after bypass surgery. He seems more short of breath and the nurses call me. Usually this is a self-limited problem, but we all worry, nonetheless. I examine John and find no new findings. New medication is ordered and John is kept in bed. His transfer to the step-down unit is delayed. Within four hours, the rhythm reverts to normal and everyone including John breathes easier. He sleeps fitfully that night, being awakened every 1-2 hours because of pain and disorientation. On one occasion, he swears that bugs are running along the walls. The nurse assures him she can't find any bugs, no matter how hard she tries. On another occasion, he awakens in a drenching sweat. By the end of day three, he is exhausted.

Day three begins slowly. John wonders if he will ever feel better. The more alert he becomes and the more he moves around, the more his chest hurts. The nurses tell him he has to move so he won't get blood clots or pneumonia, but it hurts. When he stands up he feels dizzy. He feels bloated and constipated. The meat smells bad. He would die for some ice cream or pudding.

The cardiac rehab team comes in three times that day and cheerfully tries to make him cough and move and bend and generally coerce him into recovery. Friends visit now, two or three at a time. They talk a lot and watch the television in his room. He appreciates all the company, bit it wears him out.

The nursing staff tries to teach him about "lifestyle modification" and "risk factors", but he just wants to sleep in his own bed in his own home. By the evening of the third day, he reckons he will probably survive.

Except for a nap in the waiting room, Martha hasn't slept in two days. She still has nightmares that John will die and she refuses to leave his room. A cot is brought in to accommodate her. Every time he sighs or moans, she is certain he will die, but by the afternoon of day three, she falls asleep in her chair. When she wakes up, John smiles and she returns the smile; they both know things are going to be okay.

Day four is better. John requires less pain medication. His bowels finally work and he walks more freely in the halls. Meat tastes better. He jokes with the nurses. He sleeps without night sweats. Life is looking better.

By day five, John is ready to go home. He is still sore and weak, but also thankful and optimistic. The children assure him that things are going well on the farm. He notes on the TV that hog futures are even higher today. Nurses, dietitians, chaplains, the cleaning lady and myself—we all share with him some of our words of wisdom, our medicines, or calling cards and slowly usher him toward the door.

John wants to drive home to prove he is better, but Martha says no. As he is helped gingerly into the back seat of their 1996 Ford Taurus, the world is looking better. We will check on John one last time a bit later, to see how he is progressing.

Chapter 7

How is the World Today?

I guess the way that we view the world depends upon what day of the week it is and whether we have gotten a good night's sleep. We all tend to view our individual lives as unique microcosms and not really reflecting world events around us. I think this just makes sense. How else can we tell ourselves that "I'm okay", but the world is falling apart? Conventional wisdom would have us believe that as we age we become more rigid, more narrow minded, and less willing or able to change. Politically speaking, aging does correlate with a more conservative outlook. Creativity, however, does not diminish. Many of the greatest works of art, poetry, music, and literature were written by gifted individuals in their sunset years.

During my year of research for this book, I was repeatedly heartened by the optimistic and forward looking attitudes my patients possessed. Few of them reminisced about bygone days or their past accomplishments. Rather, they wanted to talk about today and tomorrow. Didn't they realize they were close to the end? Hadn't they read the newspaper and listened to the nightly news about gloom and doom? What do they know that I don't? Maybe it is the perspective of time; they've seen this all before. If your value system is sound and your faith is strong, things do seem to work out eventually.

John Madden, the patron saint of football announcers reflected on this concept during a televised game just the other day as only John Madden can. His sidekick and straight man, Pat Sommerall asked John, "What is the difference between a mature football player and an old football player?" Without hesitation, John responded, "A mature football player still plays the game and an old football player doesn't." That says it all. Our calendar age has little to do with how old we are and how we feel about the state of the world and our lives.

I asked my patients point blank, "How is the world today?" Over half responded the world was great and getting better. About a quarter said they weren't quite sure, and only one in four thought things weren't so good. Obviously, my initial thought was that those who were most healthy would have the most positive attitudes. For them, life should be good, and so the state of the world would be "good". But, once again I was wrong. Many of the patients with the worst prognoses had the most optimistic attitudes.

I go back to Carl Brammer who illustrates what I think is going on here. He told me, "My heart problem has made me appreciate everyday and everything. I think the world is a wonderful place." Wow! When I get up each morning, I wish I could say that and mean it. I truly think that having survived adversity and having the perspective and wisdom of age leads to this attitude. We must remove ourselves from an event before we can truly appreciate its meaning. For instance, only now, fifty years after the end of World War II are we beginning to appreciate the monumental sacrifice and contribution our elders have bestowed upon us. It is that perspective of time that leads these older people to be optimistic about tomorrow, because they have seen it all before.

So many times when patients come back to see me in the office after a serious illness or event, they express gratitude and a sense that the world is now right. They may still be short of breath, they still don't like to take their medicines or restrict their salt intake, but maybe *next* year they can throw away the drugs. After all, time's a wasting! They have more important things to do like seeing their grandchildren graduate from college and critiquing those politicians who sure need straightening out.

Maybe my patients lead sheltered lives. Nearly sixty percent of them never lived anywhere but Iowa. Maybe this is a statement about the quality of life in Iowa. Every winter, when the thermometer says ten below zero and the wind is howling, I try to convince myself that the quality of life in Iowa is good. On a more practical level, maybe it is the quality of the everyday, simple things we do that count most, not the achievements that end up as plaques on walls or names on buildings. Maybe riding a tractor, mowing the lawn, getting our hands dirty, worrying about kids, and mending clothing keep us young.

Rarely did any of my patients mention personal achievement. Often they mentioned plans for tomorrow. Rather it was the fact that they had sixteen grandchildren or could still walk nine holes of golf or still played bridge with the same group of "girls" for the past forty years that seemed important.

Politics were dismissed with a sigh and a swipe of the hand, as if to erase it from their minds. Few complained openly about government or its workings. All were thankful for Medicare, but most feared that future generations would not be so lucky. Many of my patients are on five or six expensive heart medications. The cost of medications frequently takes up at least a quarter of their monthly income. We try to help them out by giving them free samples when possible, but it isn't enough. I suspect this will only get worse. Most smile gamely and say they will make ends meet.

Don Schultz, who still ran competitively at age eighty-two said something that bears repeating. "The world is all right, but the people in it create the problems." Other patients said things that were strikingly similar. I believe what they mean by this is that we are responsible for our own happiness and welfare, not anyone else.

Maxine Seaton seems to be able to make the distinction between her life and the rest of the world when she comments,

"The world as a whole is very troubled and so much rush, rush, but for me, it is a better place." I don't find that younger patients are able to dissect out the reality of "my life" from "life on the evening news" nearly so well. Because they are so rushed and stressed and bombarded with information, younger individuals don't have the luxury of time or the perspective of age. They just react. If they end up seeing me, they evidently haven't learned to react very well.

Each patient interviewed seemed to have his or her unique way of proving to themselves they were "mature players" and not just "old". Dorothy Primus does it by traveling. She told me, "I travel to prove I'm still alive." In her lifetime, she has visited all forty-eight lower states, Europe, Egypt, Turkey and Greece. She assures me there are many more exotic areas she intends to see before her story ends.

One of my patients just drives his tractor. He admits he doesn't have to drive the tractor. He has no particular place to go or chore that requires its use, but he tells me he "needs" to drive the tractor. I know what he means. He is still a player. Every time that tractor engine springs to life, he springs to life. He sees himself as the young man with the work to do and crops to plant. One day the engine won't start and he won't start and the story will end, but not today.

Many of my female patients still clean their own houses thoroughly each week. Why? That's easy. What would the neighbor think if she dropped over to borrow some sugar and there was dust on the china? Will the neighbor really be coming over? Probably not, but they just might and it's that optimism that keeps them going and keeps us all going.

A reason to get up each day, a chance to contribute, a future to think about; these things drive them on. Should I tell them to be careful, to cut back, to watch their step or should I tell them to "just do it"? (Thanks, Nike!) I tell them to keep driving and cleaning and traveling until they die. I tell them to let me worry about the details of assuring their plans will happen. Never pass up a chance to watch the sunrise on the seat of your John Deere tractor or the sunset over the Golden Gate Bridge.

I think patients with an entirely negative view toward life never make it to the exclusive over eighty club. My patients indeed see the troubles that beset our world. They have strong opinions about morals, right and wrong, and our national heritage. What they are telling me, I believe, is that it just doesn't reflect their own reality. Reality is the chance to live one more day and then another and then yet another. Reality to William Steen, age eighty-two is, "I'm very fortunate to have lived this long. I don't think I would have changed a thing in my life." Reality is Dwight Gates telling me, "One is rich if he has good health and peace of mind." Reality is Maynard Reece telling me, "I don't worry about things I have no control over. I just keep busy."

So we go back to the ever present question we each pose to ourselves every morning, "How is the world today?" Do my patients feel the way they do because they have survived the rigors of youth and work, or have they survived the rigors of life because of their attitudes? If longevity is determined merely by getting rid of infectious diseases, lowering cholesterol, and not smoking, then our aging population will continue to swell and we will probably ignore the warning signs of aggressive unbridled capitalism. On the other hand, if long life is determined by other things, not just eradicating disease, then we as a society face a much more uncertain future. The answer to this question is important. It has political, social, and financial consequences. It determines how we treat our older citizens, what value we give to their wisdom and experience, and how we best utilize their many talents. With both Medicare and Social Security issues begging to be resolved, the time to act is now. Mainstream societal values seem to be at odds with those expressed by our elders. The clock is ticking. Let's check back with John and see if he has recovered from his surgery.

Chapter 8

John Returns for Follow-up

Nearly three months have passed since John's surgery. He is sitting in my waiting room getting ready to have a treadmill test. He is in a reflective mood as he thinks back upon how he got to this point in his life.

To start, he doesn't remember much about his heart surgery. He recalls feeling weak and nauseated and scared. He thinks the surgeon bypassed his veins or was it his arteries or did they use veins to bypass arteries or arteries to bypass veins. Did they take his heart out? Did he embarrass himself? He thinks he was told what to eat and how to exercise, but when he got home, he was so glad to be alive, he just didn't care. The first thing he did when he got home from the hospital was to go out to the barn and sit on the tractor. He didn't even turn the ignition on. He just sat there. Martha finally came out and scolded him and helped him climb off the tractor. He was so weak, he almost fell and his chest ached, but it was a different kind of ache than before.

That first night home and for many subsequent nights, he slept poorly. When he turned on his side, a sharp stab would flash across his chest. When he rolled on his back, it would ever so slowly subside. Every night he would have the same nightmare; a long tube was in his throat, he couldn't talk and nobody seemed to care. He woke up with a drenching sweat and palpitations. After two weeks this seemed to subside. At first he craved fruit, then ice cream and then iced tea. As much as Martha begged him, vegetables made him sick to his stomach.

Then there was the leg. A big ugly incision extended from his groin to his ankle on his left leg. It throbbed when he tried to walk and the ankle was puffy. Martha said it reminded her of a windy river, but John didn't see the humor.

Well meaning friends came over almost every day. Everyone said how wonderful he looked. Each person examined his incision. All of his friends had expert advice for him and every pal had another pal who knew a friend or cousin who had "undergone the knife" and had his "chest cracked". John patiently put up with all the company, but he really wanted them just to leave.

Things did get better, though. By the third week after surgery, the sweats had gone away, vegetables started tasting better and his leg really started to feel like it was part of his body again. One day he decided to milk the cow. The first time he lifted the can he was sore and felt he had probably split his chest open, but he hadn't. He even drove the tractor around the yard and terrorized the unsuspecting chickens.

He also began thinking about his life a little bit differently. He was determined that he would *never* have another heart operation. Now he wasn't quite sure what all that meant, but the seed was planted. He even picked up the Bible and read a few comforting phrases. All of this seemed to come without actually thinking about it, but he knew it was the right thing to do. For the first time in his life, John seemed to savor the details. He started reading the social section of the newspaper and noted that one of his friends recently had been hospitalized. He noticed the wildflowers next to the barn. He noticed his wife knitting. He watched her cook. He didn't know exactly what was happening to him, but it was okay whatever it was.

Martha had also been changed by John's surgery. For the first week, she couldn't sleep and when he turned over in bed, she would wake up in fear that he was having a heart attack. Once she called our answering service in fear and was coached through the night.

She hovered over John. She fed him and she bathed him. She felt guilty. Had she failed as a wife? What if he dies? What will I do? But, as John improved, she improved as well. They actually became closer and closer. One night they actually sat and watched the stars and held hands—something they hadn't done in twenty years. Her friends gave her sage advice—more than she wanted. The kids called daily. Each tried to sound more concerned than the last. All meant well, but the ordeal took its toll. One night she just sat in the kitchen and cried. The break for her came when she saw John on his tractor, chasing the chickens. She smiled inwardly. She knew things were going to be all right.

John was suddenly roused from his thoughts by the treadmill technician. It was time for his treadmill test. With some trepidation, he slowly followed the technician down the stairs to the treadmill lab, removed his shirt and donned his old walking shoes. The electrocardiogram leads were pasted to his chest and he climbed on the device. He was frightened. Would he fail the test? Was he really fixed?

As he began to walk, his confidence rose; this wasn't so bad. Soon a healthy sweat appeared; he even joked with the technician. He walked for 12 ½ minutes, quite good for "an old fart", he thought. After he sat down and toweled off he made his way back to the waiting room, had a cup of cold water, turned on CNN and waited to see me.

I reviewed John's treadmill test and went over the records from his hospitalization. I noted that his weight was currently down ten pounds, his cholesterol was 178 and that his blood pressure was 130/80—all very encouraging. Now when we see patients after a life threatening illness, generally they are repentant. They come to see us with almost an attitude of confessing their sin. Part of getting well it seems, is taking responsibility for self destructive lifestyle choices. Everyone pledges they are changed, but after six months, most patients revert to their prior lifestyle choices, gain their weight back, don't exercise, and have a whole host of excuses why they can't do what they promised they would.

When I walk into the room, John seems genuinely glad to see me. He looks good. The sparkle is in his eyes. I can see that Martha has on a new dress for the occasion. She won't take her eyes off her man. They make a good team. I know that each of them needs the other and if one were to die, the other would also die within six months—that's the way it is and that's the way it should be.

John seems eager to talk. He never felt better, he says. He still can't remember much about the hospitalization, but remembers enough to convince himself he won't do this again. Martha has a list of questions written neatly on a small piece of paper, probably the same paper she used three long months ago. She wants me to tell John that he must take it easy. John wants me to tell him he is fixed and that he can return to his accustomed role as resident Superman. I side with John. I tell him *not* to slow down. I tell him this is a marathon he is running, not a sprint. His lifestyle changes must be forever, not six months. He must exercise every day, not use the salt shaker at the table, eat what Martha puts on his plate and like it. I tell him this operation has a ten year warranty; some owners abuse their bodies and return to the repair shop early, some never need an overhaul—it's up to him. I tell him if he lives to be

100, the warranty ends since I will be retired. I tell him that every year I will bug him and badger him to tow the line and I will give him holy hell if he doesn't. But, I also tell him I am proud of him and what he has already done. I really am proud of him and inwardly think if my father were still alive, I hope he would be friends with John. As John walks toward the check out desk, Martha pats my hand and smiles. I know she is happy. I hope John does well—but two more patients are ready to be seen and so it goes, John is on his own.

Chapter 9
Special People

The perspective of time is hard to beat and even harder to explain to someone who is in a hurry. As a physician for twenty-seven years, I am still in a hurry. My older patients tell me to slow down. They have been to the top of the mountain and have almost reached "home". As I slow my pace and really listen, their wisdom comes through loud and clear. Their lives reflect their values and their words are a soothing balm in an age of information overload and moral relativism. Their humor is genuine, unrehearsed, and from the heart.

As I progressed through my year long project of writing this book, I found myself chuckling at their quotes and shaking my head in disbelief at how much common sense wisdom I was privileged to share. Stoic farmers and proper housewives opened their hearts to me. Their lives became so interesting and colorful.

One of my favorite patients is Ruby Chongo; I've mentioned her before. Ruby has been married more than fifty years. She picked her husband out across the room when she was at a dance and told her friend who accompanied her that was the guy she was going to marry. She did. She claims she is "too busy to get old." "You gotta laugh," she says. She decorates her bedroom with jungle scenes, a rope, birds, and trees—the rope is "so my husband can swing on it." She likes to do things that make others happy. She likes to dress up in a funny costume for Halloween just for laughs. Last year she was Lady Godiva.

I saw Ruby in the office last week. Since her initial response to my questionnaire things have not gone so well for her. She has been hospitalized twice for heart failure and an irregular heart rhythm. It is harder for her to get around. Has her attitude changed? No way! She still greets me with a joke, a smile, and an optimistic attitude. Her "jungle mate" faithfully accompanies her. She looks short of breath to me but tells me she has a lot to do and can't waste time being sick. I hope I can help her feel better because next week she has thirty people coming over for dinner.

Sometimes you hear funny things unexpectedly and they brighten up your whole day. About six months ago Leonard Anderson made my day. I was running late seeing people in the office and Leonard was waiting patiently. When I opened the door to greet him, he could see I was stressed and distracted. He looked me straight in the eye and said, "I just don't get it, I tell them I want a *young* family internist and who do they give me, but Dr. Jack OLDS. Then I tell them I want the best heart doctor around and they give me a (Dr. David) LEMON." I cracked up. We both laughed. His comment had the desired effect. He gave me more that day than I could ever hope to give him.

As a young mother, Freda Combs, now age eighty-four, was asked by her doctor to do a favor for him. He had recently delivered a baby who evidently was abandoned and starving. He asked her for help. She cheerfully said yes and proceeded to nurse the baby back to health with her own breast milk. Why would she do such a thing? "It was the right thing to do," she said.

Alvin Anderson helped preserve our American freedom. He landed on Omaha Beach in the Normandy Invasion on D-Day, June 6, 1944 at 7:00 am and fought all through Europe. Thank you Alvin. Can we ever repay you?

John H. Peterson reminds me that "you have to live each day as if it were your last because it may be." His life has reflected that wisdom. John has traveled to fifty-eight different countries. At each stop he has made a custom of giving bubble gum to the local children and has reminded them where he comes from. He told me that the Blue Danube "really isn't that blue." He remembers being held hostage at bayonet point on a bridge somewhere in Europe for eleven hours. He remembers visiting Budapest, Hungary, three days after the overthrow of the government. He still travels; he will live life fully until he dies. I think he would make a good ambassador, so long as he didn't have to pay for all the gum.

I would be remiss if I did not tell you about Don Schultz. Don decided to take up running at the age of fifty-two. He still was running competitively at age eighty-two. In between he covered quite a bit of real estate. In fact, he figures he has logged about 19,000 miles. Don said he ran daily for six and a half years without missing a day. His slogan for competitive races is fitting—"always the oldest and almost the last." At age seventy-four he carried the torch to open the Iowa Games. At age eighty-two he ran in four 5K road races. In addition to all this running, he has worked at our hospital for fourteen years, contributing some 7,500 hours of volunteer work. Since the initial interview, Don, like Ruby, has come onto hard times. Don suffered a heart attack and mild depression. Also like Ruby, he has bounced back. He has twisted my arm into allowing him to walk briskly and to try some swimming. No matter what happens, he will live life fully until he dies.

Clark Shaw and his wife are delightful and good people; good in every sense of the word. Their children reflect their values and joy for life. On Wednesdays, Clark still goes to Crimmins Steak House to hear Dixieland Jazz. On other nights, Clark and his wife go to the back room of the Spaghetti Works Restaurant to hear old time Swing Big Band music. Their family is close and intelligent and can be funny. Not too many years ago, Clark was facing a heart valve operation. The surgeon had been discussing with the family the types of valves they might use for the operation. The two choices were basically one made from a metal product and the other a valve harvested from a pig. On the way to the operating room, Clark's youngest son reached over and whispered, "Dad, this is a great day; I see the hog market is steady." Clark remembers feeling better after that. He breezed through the surgery.

Sometimes bits of wisdom come from unexpected places and this makes them all the more real and relevant. Take the case of Barney Stenzel, age eighty-six. Barney has been a bartender for fifty-five years. He told me if he had to do his life all over again, he would live his life the same way. "I believe in treating people equally," he said. "Whether they are a banker or a ditch digger, whoever comes in first, gets served first. I've given life my best. I've kept my sense of humor. Life is what you put into it." In 1990, Barney was inducted into the Bartenders' Hall of Fame.

I've been privileged in my life to know, work with, and admire some remarkable people. One such person is Dr. Robert Hayne, age eighty-two. Bob embodies every quality that we as physicians hope to possess. Bob is a neurosurgeon. In his early years, Bob did virtually all the neurosurgery at the University of Iowa. He eventually migrated to Des Moines and never stopped operating. Intelligent, quick witted, self deprecating, he still embodies everything good about medicine. He regularly operated with extreme competence up to age eighty. I remember a few years back he had an active bleeding ulcer and developed anemia from this. Would he come into the hospital and take it easy? Oh, no! Would he even slow down for a blood transfusion? No way! As I recall, he told the gastrointestinal physicians if they wanted to transfuse some blood into him it would be okay; they could just hook him up and run it in as he operated. Bob is blessed with good genetics. His family all lived to ripe older ages. He is a lover of art. He has exercised regularly since his youth. He still has a twinkle in his eye and a shuffle in his gait and, all right, by the way, a pacemaker in his heart. I'll bet he outlives the pacemaker.

Sometimes I am struck by a patient's honesty and trust in us as physicians. I take this as a privilege to serve them and a huge responsibility not to let them down. I feel this way about my own orthopedic doctor. I want him to take on mystical powers. I want to grant to him this power. It may well be wishful thinking, but it is essential to real healing. It is called faith. Patients who live to be eighty years old have deep seated faith. It is faith in God, their family, themselves, their doctor, and in tomorrow. Cynicism and negative thinking don't mix with successful aging. Ruth Peterson said it pretty well and it bears repeating again and again. "I worry about nothing and pray about everything."

Some patients grab at your heart just because of their grit. Florence Bailey is one such lady. Florence is now ninety years old. She is a great basketball fan and loves the Chicago Bulls. She also loves the Iowa Hawkeyes. She critiques their play. Each basketball season she gives me her predictions and almost always they are correct. Last year she told me that it was a shame that John Stockton and Karl Malone didn't have a championship ring. She insisted on mowing her own lawn into her mid-eighties. Each year she asks me about my kids and how they are doing. Each year she remembers all the details. She told me I had to enjoy each day as it comes and things will work out. She also told me she truly believes we make our own heaven or hell here on earth. Once again, how can I ever give this woman what she has given me?

Hortence Harman recently died in her sleep at age ninety. In fact, I had seen her in the office a few weeks before her death. She would pass her time reading, writing, and "taking care of the 'old people' in the nursing home." She often told me, "I learned young you have to take care or yourself." Rather ironic isn't it, that she spent almost all of her later years taking care of others.

Robert Feldman proudly told me he built his own house by hand at age seventy-five—I mean "by hand". He poured all the concrete, he moved twenty tons of dirt by hand, and he wore a straw hat "when it got higher than 100 degrees Fahrenheit." It took him "about a year". He commented that his dad died while he was outside working at age ninety-three.

I am proud to know Maynard Reece. Maynard is a world renown artist who specializes in wild life illustration, especially birds. He has published in Life magazine and has been commissioned to illustrate several postage stamp designs. Maynard also plays a mean game of golf. Unfortunately, he also has heart disease. He recently underwent a coronary bypass operation which barely phased him. He is already back to work. He had a nice article written about him in the Des Moines Sunday Register, October, 1997, by John Carlson. In the article, Maynard shares with us his secrets of life. He tells us he doesn't worry about things he cannot control. He loves his work and looks forward to each day as a challenge to better his skills. He works as hard today as he ever did. It relaxes him and is the only time he is completely happy. I recently stayed at the Hotel Pattee in Perry, Iowa. Perched on a shelf in the elegant, cherrywood trimmed library was an album featuring Maynard's work. I spent a delightful time going through it. His work is truly inspiring. I believe Maynard has many more scenes to share with us in the ensuing years. I hope he never retires.

Don Schissel was my friend and colleague. He retired from practicing medicine at about age seventy-five. All of his life he epitomized the ideal physician—caring, quiet, compassionate, competent. For most of his adult life he had serious medical problems of his own with considerable pain, but he never complained or made excuses. In his waning years, he battled with prostate cancer and severe heart disease. The smile and twinkle in his eyes dulled somewhat, but never left. He once told me that early in his life he decided on his life work to be a physician. There was never any anxiety over reaching his goal. He told me his work was satisfying, stimulating, and fulfilling. He reminded me that life is filled with many ups and downs. "Without faith life is a farce," he said. He was "uncertain as to life after death, but accepted whatever would come on faith." Sadly, Don recently succumbed to his sufferings. I think Heaven has a place for Don and I know his spirit lives on in his family and many grateful patients.

I would like to close this journey with a humorous little quote I heard a few months ago from one of my sharp, intelligent patients, Rua Svenson, a former teacher. I waltzed into her examination room, a little late as usual and gave her my opening line. "Rua, how do you feel today?" Her answer is a classic. "Well, doctor," she said, "I don't know how I'm supposed to feel since I've never been this age before." Well? How should she feel?

Thank you, Rua and thanks to all my patients. You have made my twenty-seven year journey through medicine a meaningful one.

Epilogue

Carl Guenther, the inspiration for me to write this book, died recently at age eighty-six of a stroke. He lived for sixteen years after I had told him he was "too old". He often kidded me about my pronouncement when he would come to see me in the office. During those sixteen years, he lived each and every day to its fullest. He had several setbacks along the way, but each time he bounced back. Each time he would smile, thank me and diligently follow my advice. Never, never did we discuss his age. I am privileged to have learned from him.

The day that he died I went to see him. He could not speak because of the stroke, but he knew me and managed a weak smile. I grasped his hand and he gave a weak squeeze. Tears welled up in his eyes. His eyes looked sad. I think he was sad because the journey was nearly at end. I think he was also thanking me for sticking with him all those years. He died later that day. I lost a friend. I will never forget him. Thank you, Carl.

HONORING OUR GOOSE

I talked with "our goose" this morning as we shared the morning sun.

I'd been staggering and stumbling as I walked our trail, feeling old, decrepit and worn. He sat proudly, tending his broken wing and preening his beautiful body.

"How come you are not angry," I asked him, "because you can no longer fly, or mad at who or whatever has done this to you?"

He answered me, "Old lady, you too are beautiful and perhaps your wings too are getting old, but let us remember the good times we have had when we could walk, fly and soar. Those, our memories, are precious to us all. I'm happy here beside my pond, it is all I really want."

Dorothy Wilson, age 86
October, 1996

REFLECTIONS AT AGE 88

by Dorothy Peck Lynch Wilson

As I look back at all the beautiful stages
and phases of my life
and keep thinking about what is ahead for me,
I'm reminded of John Martin,
the kid next door on Rutherford.
He had been given his first two-wheeler
and had learned
quickly
how to drive it around the block,
time
and again
and again,
then back home,
up the drive
and into
the garage door
—kerplunck—
in a heap
with a joyful shout.

He had never learned to stop it,
to use the brakes.
That didn't matter to John.
It was the pleasure,
the joy,
the fun of the ride
that was worth
it all.

I guess that's how I think about my life, the joys and, of course, a few sorrows….I seem to just keep on life-cycling as John did his biking, not worrying about the brakes or how or when to stop.

Life is for loving and living.
I've done it all.
My cup runneth over.

I LEAVE YOU THE LOVE GOD GAVE ME

by Arleen Bagnall, age 87

I leave you the love God gave to me.
He's opened the door to set me free.
He welcomes me and takes me there
To the place He said he would prepare.
He'll keep on loving me I know
Beyond all ages He said so.

I hate to leave you now you know
I love you one and all,
But I must leave and go to Him
In answer to His call.

He's built a place for me up there
And it is ready now.
He blessed me much while I was here
And given me His care.
My family has been so good to me.
I've treasured every minute.

But now it's best for me to leave
I see His will is in it—
So do not grieve for long my dears
And keep your thought above
That others too might know the way
To be guided by His love—

Selected Bibliography

Ansberry, Clare. "Who's Afraid of Aging?" *The Wall Street Journal*, December 31, 1997;
pgs.1-2.

Fozard, James. *With The Passage of Time. The Baltimore Longitudinal Study of Aging*,1993;
pgs.28-49.

"In Search of the Secrets of Aging." National Institutes of Health, 1993;
pgs.1-32.

Perls, Thomas. "Acute Care Costs of the Oldest Old." *Hospital Practice*, 1997;
pgs.123-137.

Ryan, Thomas. "Aging." *American Journal of Geriatric Cardiology*, 1997; vol. 6 no. 5:
    pgs.11-15.

Weiss, Rick. "Aging, New Answers to Old Questions." *National Geographic*, 1997;
    pgs.10-31.

Clark (85) and Alice Shaw. Still lovers after 61 years.

Bernadine Keller (82).
What a nice smile

Maxine Seaton (81)
What a pretty lady!

Florence Bailey (90)
A true "Hawkeye fan"

Freda Littlejohn (81)
Twice she has died suddenly and
been resuscitated out of hospital

Dorothy Primus (83)
Has visited all lower 48 States,
Europe, and the Middle East

Edward Olney (81)
Just as tough and stubborn as he looks

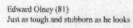

Marvin Armstrong (82)
Appreciates just being alive

CPSIA information can be obtained at www.ICGtesting.com
Printed in the USA
LVOW08s0810300516

490437LV00001B/22/P